PRETTY FOR A BLACK GIRL

A Collection of Letters, Short Stories, and Poems

By: Shanice Maxwell

Copyright @ 2024 by Shanice Maxwell

Published Independently by *House of Griot* a division of Write A Legacy, Inc.
16 Washington Ave. Suite 1416 Norwalk, CT 06856
www.WriteALegacy.club
Printed in the United States of America 2024— First Edition
Cover Illustration by: Kyle Mahoney and Kayla Phipps
Cover Design & Formatting by: Write A Legacy, Inc.
Photography by: Shaquille Simpson

All rights reserved. Except as permitted under the U.S. Copyright Act of 1976, this publication shall not be reproduced, broadcasted, rewritten, distributed, or transmitted, electronically
or copied, in any form, or stored in a database or retrieval system, without prior written permission from the author.

Library of Congress Cataloging-in-Publications Data
Pretty For A Black Girl: A Collection of Letters, Short Stories, and Poems/Shanice Maxwell ISBN 979-8-9903257-4-6 (pbk.)
ISBN 979-8-9903257-7-7 (ebook)

To every Black girl who ever looked at herself in the mirror and did not like what she saw.

To every Black girl who questions her purpose in this world.

To every Black girl who sometimes forgets she is magical.

To young Shanice.

This book is for you.

All of you.

Please know that you are more than enough.

You are the standard.

The blueprint.

The culture doesn't move without our permission.

Selah

Author's Note:

It was Super Bowl Sunday, 1995. My father was a football fanatic, but I'm sure he did not plan on watching the game from Bridgeport Hospital.

My heart stopped twice. The doctor had to perform an emergency c-section because I was choking. I came into this world a fighter. I knew what it meant to be resilient before I opened my eyes for the first time, a trait that would follow me for the rest of my life.

My parents divorced four years later due to my father's abusive nature, consistent drug use, and infidelity. This is when I first started writing. From the moment I could hold a pencil, I began writing nonstop. I filled countless notebooks with poems, essays, and short stories. Creative writing is where I found peace, strength, and healing. I remember writing an autobiography back in the 5th grade for the Young Authors Contest and discovered there was no custody battle. My father never even filed for visitation. The man who I once considered my everything wanted nothing to do with me. His words on our weekly phone calls did not match his actions back in 1999 and that caused me to question my ability to be loved. Thankfully, my mother made sure I never lacked anything. The village she and God hand-selected to help raise me reminded me daily of how smart, talented, beautiful, and blessed I was.

As the daughter of an elementary school teacher and the granddaughter of an avid reader, I grew up surrounded by literary works of the great Langston Hughes, Nikki Giovanni, Paul Laurence Dunbar, Zora Neale Hurston and more. It was my grandmother who introduced me to the world of poetry and knew I would write a book one day. My grandma was my best friend. I was so excited when she moved up from Flushing, NY to come live with us in Bridgeport, Connecticut. We shared a room, which became annoying as I moved into my preteen years, but as a young girl, I loved watching my grandmother build our library and devour books like her favorite meal.

While my grandmother would read, I would write. It was our quiet bonding time. She also was a great mediator for my mom and I. We bumped heads quite often. Mother-daughter relationships can be tricky, especially when they are riddled with traumas seen and unseen. I never felt like I was good enough or that I could do anything right. She would make comments about my weight that would send me spiraling. I had to deal with fat jokes at school and at home. I got into plenty of fights at school because of it, but I couldn't fight my own mother.

TRIGGER WARNING- SUICIDE

Not knowing how to manage these emotions, I attempted suicide three times. First, at age seven when I snuck downstairs to the garage, started my mother's car and rolled down the windows. I figured the fumes would handle it. I crawled in the back seat and laid down hoping to fall asleep. I grew impatient and cut the car off before heading back upstairs. The next time was after a string of arguments with my mother about my weight and behavior. I was about thirteen. I googled how to tie a noose on our family computer and found an old jump rope in the garage. I placed it on the shower head in the bathroom closest to the bedrooms. My grandmother must have felt like I was up to something, so she busted in before I could finish setting everything up. I now know that was God's doing.

My final attempt happened when I was in my senior year of high school. I could not understand how none of my accomplishments seemed good enough for my mom. I still felt like I could not do anything right. I was constantly being compared to other girls in my circle and she could not see how that was hurting me. Chasing after her approval was about to send me to an early grave. I figured she would be much better off without me since she didn't seem very pleased with my existence. I went into the kitchen after a huge argument with my mom and grabbed the biggest steak knife I could find in the drain. I had just finished washing the dishes. I held out my left arm, forearm facing upwards, and made a cut in the elbow crease right where I could see my veins. I still have that scar, though it has since faded a bit. When I went to move the knife to my throat, my grandmother came into the kitchen and grabbed my hand. My eyes were closed so I never saw her coming. We wrestled for the knife for a brief moment and then I gave in. She looked at me with such hurt in her eyes. She asked me to explain why I felt like this was my only option. All I could do was cry. I asked her if she was going to tell my mother and she promised me she wouldn't, but made me promise that I eventually would. When I finally was able to sit down with my mother and disclose all of this, I was twenty-two and a few months out of undergrad. My grandma had been gone for almost a year. My mother had no clue any of this was happening. My grandmother took that secret to the grave, just as she promised.

Looking back, my mother was dealing with an overwhelming amount of stress and emotions. She was able to get us both out of an unsafe environment, maintain her job as one of the best teachers the city of Bridgeport has ever employed, and hold down a household. My mom even went back to college when I was in high school to get her second masters degree. If there is one thing the women in my family do not play about, it is our education.

My grandmother was the first woman in our family to graduate from college. She attended Hampton Institute (University) and graduated in the 1940s with a degree in business. She established the standard and the rest of us have followed suit. I graduated from Cornell in 2017 without my grandma physically in the crowd. She passed away during my first week of classes senior year. That degree was for her. I then went on to complete my masters in elementary education in 2020 at Fairfield University. That degree was for me.

I had very little sense of direction about what I wanted to do career wise. As a woman of faith, I knew God already had a plan, but he was a bit slow revealing that plan to me. I taught for a few years then transitioned into the education nonprofit sector where I could combine my knowledge of labor law, organizational behavior, and HR with my passion for education and social justice. I continued to write all throughout my journey, but it wasn't until a professor in my masters program tasked us with writing a children's book as our final project for the semester that my grandmother's prophecy came back to me.

Whenever I was given a writing assignment in school, regardless of grade level, and wasn't sure how to approach it, I would fall back on my creative writing skills and write a poem. It was my safety net and had bailed me out of trouble plenty of times in various classrooms. This assignment was no different. That assignment birthed the first draft of *Pretty For A Black Girl*. I was asked to share one of the poems with my cohort. I stood at the front of the lecture hall and read For Little Black Girls With Big Names and The Darker Sister. My classmates gave me a standing ovation and my professor was off to the side sobbing. I realized at that very moment that my grandmother was right. I could actually do this author thing. It would be another four years before the thought even entered my mind again.

After a bad break up and being laid off from what I believed was my ideal job (not dream job, we don't dream of labor over here), I entered a really deep state of depression. Months went by and all I could do was sleep and cry. My girls tried to lift my spirits with brunches, vacations, concerts, parties, movies, etc. but I could not shake the feeling of failure and heartbreak. After three months of not feeling like myself, I woke up one day and decided to reclaim my joy. I turned to the one thing that always gave me comfort, poetry. I found my original copy of *Pretty For a Black Girl*, now bent and discolored from being tossed around my classroom and lost under piles of junk, and decided it was time to share it with the world.

As I do with all my passion projects, I jumped right in. I had tunnel vision. I was able to secure a six-month contract job developing social emotional learning curriculum for a non-profit, so the financial burden was temporarily lifted and allowed me to pursue this dream of fulfilling my grandmother's prophecy.

I had a meeting with a childhood friend about designing the cover on a Tuesday morning. It was so exciting! In less than thirty minutes, she had drafted up my cover art exactly how I envisioned it the night before. On Friday of that same week, I received word that my father passed away. We spent the last two years rebuilding our relationship, laughing and joking about pop culture, sharing testimonies and highlights of our weeks, and even engaged in some deep conversations around faith, romantic relationships, and me moving to a new state. I felt like he had left me, again. Only this time, he left for good. I never got to tell him about the book.

Grief tried to slow down the process, but I was determined to publish Pretty For A Black Girl. I was very intentional, yet subtle with how I honored my father and grandmother in this book. The cover has my grandma all over it. The peanut butter and banana sandwich on the table was my favorite snack that my grandma would make for me when I got home from school. I wanted the woman to be dark skinned with an afro reading a book, just like I can still picture her in our old bedroom. In Maymuna's Story, she mentions her chubby cheeks that she inherited from her father. My daddy gave me my cheeks too.

Writing is therapeutic for me, and my hope is that my words provide a sense of healing and calm for others. I don't want another child to feel what I felt growing up. I don't want them to hate their bodies, question their beauty, or feel like removing themselves from this world is the only way to make the pain go away. I want women who were once little girls to attack those harsh memories and come out whole on the other side. We are not the ones who hurt us, but healing from that hurt is our responsibility. I healed little Shanice while writing this book. I hope she's proud of me.

Table of Contents

I Am..1
- The Darker Sister............................2
- LOUD..5
- Maymuna's Story............................7
- Legs..11
- They Say (The Average Black Girl...............13
- For Little Black Girls With Big Names.........17
- Don't Touch My Hair........................22
- Legally Black....................................24
- Black Girl. Black Woman. Black Mama........26

Love...32
- No Ordinary Love............................34
- Where I Fell.....................................35
- When we make love.........................38
- A shattered heart and a scattered brain....40
- Big Girls Deserve..............................43
- But Then God Sent You....................44
- Last Wishes......................................47
- GC..51
- Push...52
- Sister Circle......................................55

Conclusion..58
Acknowledgments...........................60
About the Author............................65

To Whom It May Concern:

The problem with assuming a single story about me is your lack of fact checking. I am more than what you see in front of you. I am thee phenomenal Black woman. I am the darker sister who refuses to sit in the kitchen when company comes. I am the loud one in the group. The bad, fat Black girl. I am the hope and dream of the slave. I am the teacher I wish I had growing up.

Dr. Kimberlé Crenshaw coined the phrase *intersectionality* 30 something years ago and you still don't get it. I have layers and one does not come before the other. I am both Black and woman, simultaneously. Multifaceted. Multitalented. You can't box me in. I am every woman, but not your Superwoman.

Respectfully Submitted,
THAT Black Girl

I Am

The Darker Sister

The Blacker the berry,
the sweeter the juice,
right?

Do Pac lyrics still apply
if the rest of my family is light?

I'm the only one
bearing this badge
my daddy calls it an honor

But I didn't ask for this

Look at me!
Nobody asks for this!

A recessive trait
or
maybe
it was a mutation

I hate seeing my mother cry
as I question her creation

Possibly adoption?

Weren't there any other colors?
God,
this was really your best option?

My teacher often calls me pretty
and later adds intelligent
But EXTRA! EXTRA! READ ALL ABOUT IT!
"You're pretty for a Black girl," is NOT a
compliment!

We took class photos the other day
and when I showed my mom the proofs,
she called the photographer incompetent

A dark shadow was cast
right where I was standing
A simple alteration of the light
wouldn't have been that demanding

I just want her to be seen!
My mom screamed

I look at myself in the mirror
Well, maybe they will
with this new lightening cream

I am the darker sister
if you couldn't already tell

I'm the outlier in my family
and in my class as well

My grandma is the only one
whose skin kind of looks like mine

Hers glistens like the moon
against the New York skyline

She wears it
with such elegance
and grace
One day
I hope to carry mine this way
One day

LOUD

They tell me to let freedom ring,
yet place silencers over their ears
They make us sing their songs
before we play their sports
Always the players
Never the owners

They force me to read
their version of what really happened,
conveniently leaving out their wrongdoings
and shunning me from the truth

Speak truth to power though
That's what Pastor always says

Freedom with restrictions,
a shame isn't it

Wait til she finds out our skin is the reason because of it!

They scare me into thinking they have dominion over me
Little do they know
they'll have to re-think America because of me

They place false images in front of me
And trick me into believing that is beautiful
Well I, too, am beautiful America

I am beautiful
and loud
and strong

My heart beats as loud as my ancestors' drums
And you will never be able to silence me
You call me loud
but it's because you've silenced me

The darker sister you left out in the sun
has found her voice
This loud Black girl
will always speak up
especially
when you've left her no choice

Maymuna's Story

I had to fight a kid in class today. He kept tugging on my hijab. It took me years to get it just right to where it forms my face in a way that doesn't make me look like a blowfish. I inherited my chubby cheeks from my father.

"Stop!" I hollered. I could feel the chiffon layers slipping back behind my ears. The rest of the class started to laugh and some even joined in on the taunting. I moved my seat and tried to ignore them. The teacher only stepped out of the room for a brief moment, but it felt like an eternity. He kept tugging. This time, he ripped it. "Terrorist!," he screamed as he spit on me. I could feel the hatred of his ancestors as it dripped down my cheek. That's when I lost it.

I don't remember anything after that. I guess I must've blacked out. All I know is I am now in the principal's office waiting for my parents to come. I'll probably get sent home. I know Mr. Dewey doesn't tolerate fighting. I wish they would hurry up. The steel chairs in here are hard and cold. I can't get comfortable on these things. I hope I landed a few good punches. There are rips in my lavender chiffon hijab, my favorite one. It was a gift from my older sister. Yeah, I had to make Tony pay for this and I'm not talking about money. That little boy was about to feel my wrath.

I can hear my mom now, complaining about my lack of temperance as a young lady and how Allah says we should show love, not hate, even to those who do not show love to us. My father will probably give me a high five and then lecture me about fighting in school.

I wonder if Tony got his parents called too. I slowly open the door and peek outside, but I don't see him. I slam the door in total disbelief. Typical! Blame the Somalian girl, the victim! I plan my entire argument in my head, preparing for the principal, my parents, and Tony. Time must've gotten away from me because what seemed like only 10 minutes was really 45 and in walk my parents and the principal. I stand up and begin to explain myself when Mr. Dewey, my principal, puts his hand in the air as if to silence me and begins to apologize. He tells me Tony has been suspended effective immediately and offers his office as a safe space whenever I need it.

Mom leans over and whispers in my ear, "See Maymuna, people are understanding. Times are changing." Dad leans over and whispers in my other ear and says, "I hope you sent him to the nurse." I giggled and shook the principal's hand. "I'll see you on Monday, Maymuna. You will have detention for fighting as we do not condone that behavior." Detention beats suspension any day so I smile and say, "Bright and early!"

I kiss my parents and head back to class. Before I exit the room, my mom hands me a new hijab. I smile at her and run to the bathroom to change. I take my time removing the ripped one. Anger seeps into my veins as I unwrap each layer. I handle it delicately, for it is sacred after all. It has been traumatized enough for one day. I gently fold it and place it on the ledge right above the sink. I take three deep and intentional breaths before putting on the one my mother handed me. Once I get it just right, I look into the mirror and smile at my reflection.
That's better.

I pick up my lavender hijab and walk out the bathroom. I stop by my locker before returning to class to place it at the top for safe keeping.

When I return to the room, my teacher is reading my favorite book, <u>Copper Sun</u> by Sharon Draper. My classmates look shocked to see me return so quickly. The teacher even stutters over her words once she sees my face. I take another deep breath and take my seat in the front. I adjust my hijab, fix my posture, and listen intently as my teacher continues to read.

"We must welcome our guests, then, Amari. We would never judge people simply by how they looked—that would be uncivilized…"

I hope everyone heard that.

Legs

Catch up Reid! Let's go! Hustle! Move those legs!

I hate gym. I hate sports. And I definitely hate my dad for making me try out for basketball. He says, "With legs like those, you're going to make us rich! My little Maya Moore." I don't even know who that is.

I am not a baller, but apparently my legs say otherwise. I've been slowly embracing them because I hated them all through middle school. Kids called me mean names like daddy long legs and giraffe girl. So what if I towered over most of them! That doesn't make me a weirdo. It doesn't automatically make me a NCAA prospect either.

Quiet as it's kept, I want to be a dancer. I want to be the next Misty Copeland! I want to go to Juilliard, study under the great Judith Jamison, and join the Alvin Ailey Dance Company! I want the solo in a production with the Dance Theatre of Harlem. I do not want to run up and down a court dribbling a ball.

These legs are not those of a baller. These are the legs of a dancer. I tell stories with them. These legs work in unison with the rest of my body to bring visions to life.

I want to tell stories of pain, pride, and victory. These legs sing symphonies of strength, fight, and struggle. They plié with perseverance and pirouette through pressure. These legs, my legs, are the legs of a griot.

They Say (The Average Black Girl)

They say the average black girl is loud. She's aggressive and overbearing. Slightly illiterate with several sides of ghetto. That's what *they* say. But the Black girls I know! Man listen! The Black girls I know own their OWN TV network. They are Olympic gold medalists and the greatest athletes of all time.

I'm told the average Black girl is mean. "She's so angry. Oh! But not you Yara. You're not like *them*," they say. "Them?" I ask.
"You know! Them! Those Black girls."

Would someone please tell me who "them" is? Because the average Black girls that I know are angry for a reason. The average Black girls I know are sick and tired of being sick and tired. These Black girls grow up to become Black women who show out in record numbers every election season attempting to save us all for the millionth time.

Imagine that. One of the last groups to receive the right to vote having the power to shift such a huge decision. And we are still the most disrespected persons in America.

They say I'm so well spoken as if English is so difficult for someone who was born and educated in this country. Maybe it's because I got into that fancy honors program. I hear I'm the only one who looks like me in there. Maybe that's why they don't consider me the average Black girl.

But that shouldn't even matter. Because the average Black girl I know was the only First Lady to hold two Ivy League degrees. The Black girls I know are inventors, engineers, mathematicians, astronauts and more.

Standing 5 feet 3 inches off the ground dressed in my Catholic school uniform, I stare into the floor length mirror in my mother's room trying to figure out why I'm not seen like the rest of the Black girls at school.

My mother peeks her head in and questions my presence in her room. Her olive toned skin is providing the perfect landing spot for the strip of sunlight that is pressing its way through the blinds. Her mid-length, dirty blonde hair sits on her shoulders, curled upwards as if her ends are pointing at me. Yes, my mother is white. Don't stop reading! Come back here!

Now that you have discovered this part of my identity, I hope you can better understand my struggle. I know it is easy to ignore the biracial experience and joke about how we only have one set of Black grandparents or tell us we can only celebrate Black History Month during the last half of February. I giggle out of nervousness, not agreement.

I am still a Black girl. Aren't I? I mean, yes. My skin is lighter and my curls are looser, but there is no cookie cutter factory for Black girls. We defy gravity with our hair and magic rests in our complexions. ALL of our complexions.

The Black girls I know remind me of my heritage. They call me cousin, bonded by our fathers' friendship, some bonded by our blood. They continuously beat the odds when the deck was stacked against them before they were formed in their mother's womb. The Black girls Jesus hand selected to give voice to generations, sing melodic tunes during revolutions, and recite poetic prophecies that cause a hush to fall over inauguration crowds. I come from those Black girls.

So *they* aren't wrong. I'm not the average Black girl. I can only aspire to be.

For Little Black Girls With Big Names

Whenever someone asks me the story behind my name,
I never know how to answer

There is no special story to be told
It lacks heart, swag, and soul
But I like to think my mama meant for it to be
compassionate, rich, and bold

You have to emphasize the SHA
You know, say it with some passion!
Just like it rolls off my mother's tongue
with her Brooklyn born accent

Do you ever get tired of people mispronouncing your name,
then you correct them and they shrug as if it's all the same?

It's foreign to them
so they blame it on illiteracy,
never creativity,
or maybe even history

They clown us
for they do not understand

Like my girl Quvenzhané
A few silent letters
And an 'e' marked with an accent
Preferably pronounced with the twang of a
Louisiana accent

I remember the days
when I prayed
my mother would change my name
I would get in front of people
and alter the way I said it
Try to soften the blow
To decrease the shame

It broke my mother's heart
I could see it in her eyes
Longing for the day her baby girl would realize
The power she possessed
something she has that nobody can take away

I can see it now
But I didn't always feel this way

My mother must have known
I'd be a leader someday
Even though there were times

I thought my name was too ghetto to say

Why couldn't it be something simple
and pretty
like Ashley or Alexis
But my mother must have known
I needed something a tad more
rough around the edges
to possess this
spirit of resistance
will to fight
And the mind to collectively strategize

So let me take a moment to apologize
Mommy, you gave me a name I now wear proudly
I'm sorry for the moments where I undoubtedly
Questioned your choices and viewed it as shame
Of having to forever bear what I considered to be a ghetto ass name

With Hebrew origins,
Shanice means God is gracious
and merciful
I now see it wasn't haphazard,
it was purposeful

And you!
Maybe you're a warrior

like Yaa Asantewaa!
Or your name rhymes with royalty
like Nefertiti or Cleopatra

You,
little Black girl with the big name,
are the chosen one

You are so special
and I hope you see
that there isn't another girl in the world
like you or me

So find out what your name means
and embrace it
It'll give you strength to face it

All of the world's pressures
and when you feel as if
you don't measure
up the ante
remember who you are
and what's at stake

our history
our culture
our memories
all rooted in your names

No more limiting who we are
to the first letter and a period
Yes, I know discrimination
based on names is serious
But sign your full name anyway
Right there on that line
let it take up space
on the magazine covers,
marquees,
and bylines

and if someone fails
to pronounce it correctly
make sure to give your neck a swirl
add a tongue pop for some flair
run your hand full of acrylic nails
right through your hair
look them dead in the eyes and say
it's pronounced this way
say it right or don't bother saying it at all

Don't Touch My Hair

My crown and glory
My mane

No, you cannot touch it

See with your eyes, never your hands
It glistens in the day and night
like the sun and moon kissed each strand

My hair is a form of expression
I chopped it during my depression
I braid it during a recession
It forgave me for that relaxer phase
what a blessing

3C hair
with all of the curl and flair
When I pull them
the curls bounce back

NO YOU MAY NOT TRY IT FOR YOURSELF!

And yes,
I am aware that this is magic your hair lacks

I change my hair monthly

this is true
But it does not alter my face
so stop asking,
"Girl, is that you?"

Yes, hello!
How do you do?
I bought new clothes and jewelry too.

But you don't invite your hands to these extremities
Do you even notice how I flinch
as your hand gets closer to my head?
I shrink as you grip my braids
They no longer feel like mine

I guess next time
I'll have to walk around with a sign:

DON'T TOUCH MY HAIR!

Legally Black

We gave birth to the world
and it still wasn't enough

The economy was built
on our bruised backs
and hurtin' hips

We have carried
the mediocre
melanin deficient
for centuries

All while
grabbing degrees,
curing diseases,
raising families,
ours and yours,
healing communities,
fighting systems designed for our demise
and saving generations

Superman can't do what we do
And we still find time to look good doing it

You look shocked

How do they do it all
you ask
We're Black women.

What, like it's hard?

Black Girl. Black Woman. Black Mama.

One day
I'll walk my child to the bus stop
and wave goodbye as it pulls off
And as the stop sign folds in
and the flashing lights cease,
as the bus pulls away from the curb
and moves back into traffic,
the butterflies in my stomach will die

The anticipation of this day
will quickly turn to fear
and I won't be able to stop pacing
I'll spend my entire day
wondering what happened

Will the teacher be
on the right side of justice
or will they succumb
to the pressures of administration
Will my pride and joy be forced
to have DuBois's double consciousness
before choosing her cubby?

Will my precious gift have to figure out
how to navigate microaggressions
before he experiences music class?

Will they be sent to the principal's office
for speaking out of turn
because the teacher assumed
everyone knew to raise their hand
and wait to be called on?

The playground worries me
because of my own stories
She's built like me
and though I tell her she's beautiful
all of her is beautiful
fat jokes from the lips of your peers
still cut deep
My scars are still there
Scars I wear so my child won't have to.

As she gets off the bus,
as he runs into my arms,
as they hold my hand
and we walk back home,
I take a deep breath
and exhale the whispers of anxiety

I ask them,
"How was your first day of school?"
I clench my jaw as I await their response.
I fight to stay positive

and silence the dark thoughts that quickly infiltrate
my mind
I feel like they're taking too long to answer.

Mommy!
I brace myself.

There were so many kids
and the school is so big!
My teachers are really nice too!
We watched videos
about letters and numbers.
I can count to 100, want to see?
My daughter
The numbers queen

I exhale
and find peace awaiting me
I'm glad the shadow that haunts me
has not yet consumed her

Her innocence standing guard
at the gate of her eagerness to learn
completely unaware
of the shortcomings
I'll have to address
and the mental and spiritual wounds
I'll have to mend

due to inadequate practices,
racist systems,
and inevitable experiences.

I will constantly
swallow the words
of an apology
for the mess
that is our education system
as if I single handedly
constructed its being

The duality of being the child
of an educator
who became an educator
informs my decisions
It's also why I worry for my future children
I know I strive to arm my students
for battles beyond the classroom,
but will their teachers do the same?

Will they stand up
or shrink
when my son needs them most?
Will they make conscious decisions
to check their bias
before addressing my daughter
about her "sassy attitude"

or mistake my son
for another student
with no other reasoning
besides being tall and Black

Will you fight for them a little harder
because they look like you?
Or will you be harder on them
because they could pass for yours?
Is excellence the expectation
or will trying their best be good enough?

I tote the line between effort is commendable
and we have to be better than ok
because of who we are

Do you?
Will you?
What will you do when my child,
my greatest creation,
is in your classroom?
I hope you speak life
as I do.

I will breathe strength down her spine,
I hope you will too.
I will oil his scalp with curiosity,

instructing him to massage it in
throughout the day
I hope you encourage him
as droplets end up on your floor

Still,
I pray my baby's first day is blessed
I pray her first day is colorful
and loud
and playful
and challenging
I pray his first day
is boisterous and vivacious!
I pray they never have a day
like the days I've had.

Love

No Ordinary Love

It's like I've known you my whole life
You see parts of me
I dedicated myself
to hiding,
suppressing

You've unearthed versions of me
my own mother hasn't seen
You strike nerves I never knew I had
You plant seeds in a garden
I closed off from visitors years ago

It's like you enjoy
ignoring red flags
and running red lights

You've sat me down like a child
Forced me to have tough conversations
Refuse to let me run from myself any longer
It's almost as if you love me

You hold the mirror
up to my face
and tell me all the things
you see
things you love

You kiss my tears
and a shock goes through my body
It warms me from the inside
calms my fears
quiets my doubts
and returns my heart back to its resting rate

In your arms
I've found my resting place
This is no ordinary love
Because you don't look like
the man in my dream
In fact, you don't look like a man at all

You look like me

Where I Fell

ya know,
i think joy lives
in the crevice of your smile
it seeps onto my lips
and infects my soul
whenever we kiss
dame besos

i've been struggling
to hold onto my own
but yours be
selfless
giving
like you

i don't know how i got here
smiling at the thought of you
blushing at the sight of you
butterflies swarming in my gut
at the mention of your name

you must be magic
black magic
the kind daddy warned me about
a mythical being who specializes
in safe spaces for broken hearts to land

but they be broken too

i don't know how I got here
i did exactly what I promised myself
i wouldn't do
i fell

knees bruised by your gentle spirit
arms heavy with your tears
back sore from your compassion
chest caved in from your emotional intelligence

a fight i thought
i was player enough to win
but when that Jones came down,
it hurt like a mother fucker
and i fell

and i don't think
i'm ready to stand up
standing is walking's predecessor
and unless i'm going in your direction,
i think i'll just stay here
lay here
on the ground for a while

the view from down here
on my back is
everything

When we make love ...

I want it to feel like a medley of love poems written by our favorite storytellers
I want it to sound like our favorite love songs on a continuous loop
I want it to feel like the first embrace after being deprived of human interaction for months

I want it to sound like Heaven is rejoicing
I want it to be pleasing in His eyes
I want it to be equal,
mutual,
a partnership
I want us to make love to each other

When we make love,
I want it to draw attention
I want it slow so I can feel every piece of you
I want your eyes open and the lights on
so you don't miss a part of me

I want eye contact
so we both know when the time comes
I want it right when
the moon and the sun change shifts
so night knows it wasn't the only thing broken

When we finally make love,
the moans echoing in the air
will remind us that the wait was worth it
It'll feel like the stars
aligned just for this moment
and the universe paused long enough
just for us to experience love

A shattered heart and a scattered brain

Did you mean any of it?
Every I love you
that I can recall
is so faint now
I close my eyes
and silence those around me
I can still hear you
they are wrapped up in the winds whispers

Was it all a lie?
Every forehead kiss
I now want to scrub loose
Maybe if I burn the areas where you touched me
your memory will leave

I am constantly walking through a revolving door
meeting anger,
sadness,
and tears
on the other side

You make me out to be the villain
conveniently neglecting
your own faults in this story

YOU WEREN'T PERFECT EITHER!

But I never expected you to be
I was further along
in my healing journey than you
so I was already hip to it
I knew not to make homes out of people
when my spirit was not right

You should've left me alone
The damage caused by those before me
fell from your lips at the most awkward times
I wanted to love you past that pain,
but you felt comfortable in it
You wore your scars like Purple Hearts
and I couldn't compete with ghosts

Your lazy attempts at self work
were insulting to my daily rituals
of loving you

In spite of everything
I showed you grace
just like our Heavenly Father
and you showed me the door

You expected me to heal you
that wasn't fair

You cannot place
your emotional burdens
on your partner
and call it love
Who taught you that?

Big Girls Deserve

The big girl deserves love too
Her size gives him something to hold onto
Gives her hands somewhere to explore
My back is wide and my man is fine
My girl is tall and thin
And she still be mine
The big girl deserves love too
Completely
Genuinely
A Godly love
A love befitting of her
Flattering
A love sold only in her size

But Then God Sent You

To the Chocolate Man Who Made Me Realize I Was Capable of Love,

When I was a junior in college, my friends and I made a list. We each wrote down all the characteristics we wanted in a future partner/husband. Looks, intelligence, religion, everything. I found my list around February and I prayed over it. I began praying for my future husband too. I prayed for his health, his well being, his family, his job, his patience, peace, and his heart. I prayed for his protection and continued spiritual, emotional, mental, and physical growth until we found each other. Every man I came across from that point on, I questioned God's plan. Were our paths crossing just because or was there a true purpose? I realized I was over thinking and began to have a prayer rooted in one of my favorite poems entitled I Will Wait For You. This poem lingered in my heart for months, but then God sent you.

He opened my eyes to see you and it was like having vision for the first time in years. Everything looked different, sounded clearer, shined brighter and made more sense. And it's funny, at that moment, that list I made seemed irrelevant. While there were some aspects of it you had, there were some you didn't and I was completely okay with that. People mentioned those things to me in the beginning. and I was at such a level of peace with our relationship that I felt comfortable ignoring them and sharing how you changed me for the better in such a short amount of time. They could see the joy in my walk, the peace on my face, and the genuine glow surrounding me. Something only you and the Lord could do.

Thank you for continuing to keep joy in my walk, peace on my face, and a glow around me. You've also refueled my belief in love and reminded me I am capable of being loved. Men have made me feel the opposite, all starting with my father. Two have even told me I am hard to love, and as strong, grounded and independent as I am, I started believing it.

Thank you for seeing me for who I am and choosing to love me anyway. Love is a verb so it requires action. You have seen me in my most vulnerable state and you still decide to love me. Thank you for choosing love and thank you for choosing me to love. Thank you for allowing me to love you back. Thank you for being in tune with my emotions and knowing when my energy is off. Thank you for pushing me to communicate those things. Thank you for allowing God to use you. Thank you for being persistent as you try to figure out what you want your life to look like. Your hustle inspires me. I am becoming a better woman because of you. I love you to life.

                Love,
                Sha

Last Wishes

Tell her I'm sorry
for leaving my fingerprints along your spine
It's just kinda hard to accept
that you're no longer mine

Tell her I'm sorry about my fragrance
being wrapped up in your sheets
and the fact that our heartbeats
are still so perfectly in sync

Tell her I'm sorry for my laugh
that still lingers in the air
And I'm sorry for my delicate hand's imprint
in the waves of your hair

Tell her I apologize for the pieces
of myself that I left
tucked all the way in the back
of our closet
your closet
the closet

I didn't leave them on purpose,
at least I don't think I did
Just make sure she doesn't touch them

and sell them for the highest bid

The items I left behind:
My heart,
my body,
and my soul
I left each one with your name
written on them in bold
with ink made of gold

And you probably tried to remove them
erase them from your memory
but you touched them
and in your hands
they fit so perfectly

Your face began to crack
into that crescent shape I always admired
and you start to remember everything
about me you first desired
those things that prompted you to inquire

but before you backslide,
she puts her hand on your back side
and you drop those things
that belong to me

and now she's left wondering
the same thing
if and when
you'll return to touch them again
and if you ever really meant it
when you called me Heaven sent

Do you call her that too?
Does she know how close we still are?
Does she hate it?

Does she loathe the fact
that we both tug on each other's heart strings
like we have one second to ring the bell
at the top of the rope in gym class?

Does she know I spent the night
in your bed the other day
in her absence
and that we didn't just cuddle?
Did you tell her?!

Did you tell her about
our late night conversations about religion?
About our families
and childhood memories
About our future
together

children included
but reality apparently sold separately

Does she know that you
continuously look out for me,
doing more than what
"just a friend" would do?

Is she aware
that when I tell you I love you,
you say it back?

If you don't tell her anything else,
tell her this
Make sure you tell the new girl
I'm sorry

GC

To the group chats that
give me a soft space to land
provide me with reassurance
when I think I'm buggin'
are down to ride out
when that man tries me
The chats that
let me talk my shit
cry and complain
hold space for my grief
share praise reports
to keep my spirits lifted
To the group chats that
go quiet when we are busy
finding our way
may we always find our way back
to you
to the chat
where our heart is
it's safe
here
back home

Push

Nana always said keep your legs closed and your mouth shut. But I slipped up one night. I got into bed with three different partners and now I'm pregnant. Strength has been around the longest. I met him when I was 4 amid all the drama with my parents.

Now, Perseverance, Percy for short, we went to college together. I tried to ignore him but he never left my side. Attached at my hip, but I grew to like his company.

Percy has this cousin, though. His name is Determination. I could see the resemblance. That was a smooth somebody right there. A hustler. Never took no for an answer. He always knew what to say, how to say it, and timed it perfectly. I hope this baby has a little piece of each of them.

As beautiful as I know this baby will be, I'm just not ready. I'm not ready to receive shameful stares from all of you. Looking your nose down at me in judgment and disgust. I'm really dreading telling my mama. How will I tell my mother that I went and got myself pregnant? No marriage, no house. However, to my surprise, she was already aware.

You see, this baby that is inside of me doesn't just grow for 9 months. It's been growing, rolling around, transforming for almost 30 years. Her kicks are no longer playful. They hurt like hell because she is beyond ready to push her way to the light.

Mommy, I want to see. Mommy, I want to experience life. Mommy, I want the world to know who I am and what I can do. Mommy, mommy, mommy! Are you listening to me?

    I ignore my own child's cries because I'm not ready for this type of responsibility. Then I remember the prolific prophet said something so profound, "It's not on you, it's in you." So let me go get ready. I send a quick prayer up to Heaven. I hope God can hear me. I haven't been the most obedient lately. Y'all think God holds grudges?
    I walk into a room and notice I'm not alone. I'm not the only one here with a baby bump. Some of y'all look like you're about to pop any minute now! A nurse steps forward. She's dressed in all white and maybe I'm trippin', but I think I saw wings coming out of her back.
    She is looking for a volunteer to be induced. We all look around the room, terrified. Nobody wants to go into labor first. Then a voice from above says, "Go ahead and birth your babies. They all will be friends and share a name." We all

hold hands, trembling and afraid. Together, we push. God signs their birth certificates with His sacred breath and spells out *possibility*.

Sister Circle

Girl,
do you know who you are?
Like really know who you are?

You are the glue that holds together households
The anchor that stabilizes friend groups
A glimmer of hope in the midst of the storm

Sometimes,
you are the eye of the hurricane
Unleashing warranted and necessary havoc
Reminding mediocrity and stupidity
that they have no place here

Sis,
you are the embodiment of love
The creator of life
The backbone,
collarbone,
and femur
so those kids can walk around upright

You are yesterday's mistakes
today's lessons
and tomorrow's potential

You are light
You stand taller than oak trees in summertime
You are the remnants of the strange fruit
that would hang lifeless

You are the reincarnation of God's promises
to his chosen generation

A vision of sisterhood
warm
expandable
but not indestructible
Just because you are magical
doesn't mean you aren't human

Remember to nourish yourself
as you pour into the empty cups of others
Remember to create more seats at the table
Remember to get up from that table
when you are no longer being served
Remember everything
your grandmother taught you

Baby girl,
remember who and whose you are

Black girl
Black woman

You are enough
You are the standard
You are the blueprint
Everyone else is just a partial copy,
a shallow duplicate

Continue to grow
Continue to shine
Learn and develop
in your own time

God's promises to you
are still yes and amen
Take solace in that
Find rest in those words
You are not forgotten
You are Her greatest work

Selah

Hey Sis,

My favorite modern day poet, Jasmine Mans, once said, "Your poem doesn't start until you tell the truth." The issue with telling the truth is that it is never pretty or neat. It's as ugly as they come, messy, and loud. The truth will not go unnoticed. It will barge into rooms and uproot everything. So it's better to lead with it than hide it away and secretly pray it remains unfound.

My truth found its way into a book, this book. What started off as a children's book assignment emerged as a coming of age story through poetic prose. A healing space for wounded souls. My prayer is that this will be the catalyst for some breakthroughs, the launching pad for breaking generational trauma cycles and curses, and the foundation for rebirth for all who seek it. Healing is possible and it has no deadline. It is something we will continuously chase, but it is attainable. You just have to start.

I am so proud of the women we are today. In the same breath, I can acknowledge the hurt, loss, sacrifice, trials and triumph that got us to this point. While this journey to and through womanhood has not been easy, it has been worth it. The journey reflected in these pages does not solely belong to me, but to anyone who can relate. Just remember, it takes a village, so be mindful of the circle you build around you. We are community oriented creatures. This work cannot be done solely in isolation.

I would love to hear your thoughts and personal testimonies about *Pretty For A Black Girl*. I am also open to interviews, podcast appearances, and poetry readings. Feel free to connect with me on social media for uplifting quotes and testimonials. You are now part of my sister circle and I would be honored to be a member of yours.

Until next time, pretty girl!
                Love,
                Sha

        All inquiries can be emailed to:
        thehouseofgriot@gmail.com

           Follow me on Instagram:
                @shayyymaxxx

Acknowledgements

Do me a favor. Read this with Thank You by Bow Wow and Jagged Edge playing in the background. That kept playing in my head as I wrote this.

Black women have continuously held me when I didn't have the strength to stand on my own, which is why my first book had to be an outpouring of love to and for them. I would not have made it through my toughest seasons without Black women. Family, friends, sorors, play aunties, sisters, and cousins, thank you all for showing up the way you do. You have continuously stood in the gap, joined me in the trenches, and pulled me up. You have dusted me off and reminded me who I am more times than I can count.

To my mother, we may not have always got it right, but we always found our way. You gifted me something more precious than gold and for that, I will always be grateful. You introduced me to Jesus and that is the best step you took on your parenting journey. You taught me the importance of faith, a consistent prayer life, and trusting God's plan. When all else failed, I knew I could always come back home to you and God where you'd be sitting at the edge of the bed with your arms wide open ready to embrace me.

I love you mommy. Thank you for every decision you made that got me to this point. Thank you for being a faithful servant of the Lord and stepping up to the challenge of being a parent, my parent. Job well done.

To my girls! Pieces of my heart. My sisters by choice. I cannot thank you enough for showing up for me in multiple capacities. Our paths did not cross by happenstance. God is so intentional. From my childhood besties, my soul sister, and my camp siblings, to my linesisters and sorors, thank you a million times over for pouring into me. You sewed into me when my faith was weak and grief was aiming to take me out. My future children have the coolest aunties ever. I hope you all know how special you are. I love bragging about my circle. The it girls! I love each and every one of you. I pray you saw yourselves in these pages. You inspired these words. This is my gift to you.

To my family and friends who financially poured into me to make this possible, thank you so much. With the cost of everything constantly rising, I was honored and humble when you fulfilled my request for donations to publish my book in place of birthday and Christmas presents. May you see the fruits of your generosity and be proud. You are part of this legacy.

Kayla: I came to you with my vision and you embraced it wholeheartedly. You graciously agreed to design my cover and mocked it up right there in our first meeting. You knew how important the cover was to me and you made it happen! Even in the midst of your own health challenges, you did not forget me. Thank you, my sister, for believing in my vision and supporting my dream. I love you forever.

To those who inspired my love poems, may you accept my words and attempt to immortalize you as a thank you. I learned so much about love from each of you. I will take those lessons with me as I move forward in love and life. I wish you all nothing but the best as you continue to navigate the complexities of love. May you take the lessons I taught you with you into your next phases. Any love I gave you is yours to keep. You're welcome.

And finally, to my council: Alexis, Porsha, and Ms. Gina. The three of you pushed, stretched, and challenged me to embrace the editing process. Lex, you were the final push I needed to take this leap of faith. You've always encouraged me, but that conversation in the tea shop that day changed everything. Porsha, I've always admired your grace and diction. I knew you would push me to dig deeper and really tell this story, the good, the bad, and the ugly. You challenged me to make these words real and have the reader feel what I'm saying. Thank you, sis. Ms. Gina, I don't remember life without you. You have been an essential part of my village since I met you at the sweet age of five at Jada's birthday party. Thank you for sewing into this project. Thank you for always seeing me in a way I am never quite ready to experience for myself. You all took the time to read and provide feedback on what has now become just part of PFABG. I couldn't divulge everything! Thank you for every suggestion and question. Thank you for your honesty. Thank you for taking the time to be part of this process. Thank you for contributing to this legacy. I hope one day I can return the favor.

Grandma.
Daddy.
We did it.

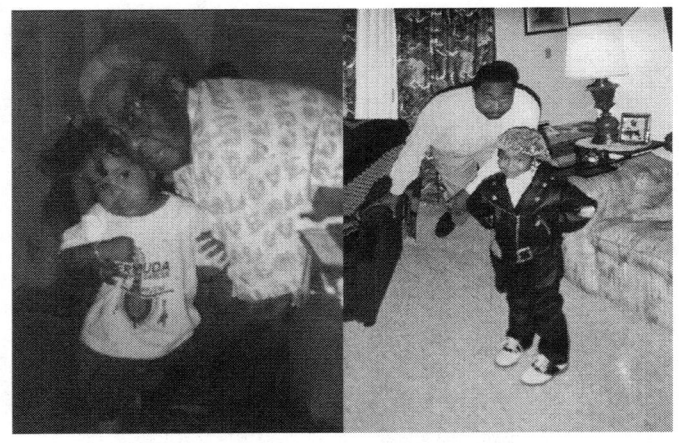

In loving memory of Carol McGhee and Bruce Maxwell.
May a copy reach you both in Heaven's library.

About the Author

Shanice Maxwell is an educator from Bridgeport, Connecticut. As the daughter of a teacher, Shanice grew up surrounded by the literary works of the great Langston Hughes, Nikki Giovanni, Paul Laurence Dunbar, and more. It was her grandmother who introduced her to the world of poetry and knew she would write a book one day. From the moment she could hold a pencil, Shanice would go on to fill countless notebooks with poems, essays, and short stories. Creative writing is where she found peace, strength, and healing. It is Shanice's hope that her writing does the same for others. From the streets of Bridgeport, CT to the lecture halls of Cornell University, Shanice held onto her core values of education, faith, and persistence. *Pretty for a Black Girl: A Collection of Letters, Short Stories, and Poems* is Shanice's writing debut.

Made in the USA
Las Vegas, NV
06 April 2024